INTRODUCING DINOSAURS

APATOSAURUS

BY SUSAN H. GRAY · ILLUSTRATED BY ROBERT SQUIER

The Child's World

Published in the United States of America by The Child's World®
1980 Lookout Drive • Mankato, MN 56003-1705
800-599-READ • www.childsworld.com

ACKNOWLEDGMENTS
The Child's World®: Mary Berendes, Publishing Director
The Design Lab: Kathleen Petelinsek, Art Direction and Design;
Victoria Stanley and Anna Petelinsek, Page Production
Editorial Directions: E. Russell Primm, Editor; Lucia Raatma, Copy Editor;
Dina Rubin, Proofreader; Tim Griffin, Indexer

PHOTO CREDITS
©Jklune/Dreamstime.com: cover, 2–3; ©AMNH Photo Studio/American
Museum of Natural History: 6; ©A. J. Copley/Visuals Unlimited, Inc.: 8;
© Michael Pettigrew/iStock: 12–13; ©Francois Gohier/Photo Researchers,
Inc.: 14–15; © AMNH Photo Studio/American Museum of Natural History:
16 (top); ©Francois Gohier/Photo Researchers, Inc.: 16–17; ©Ben Klaffke: 19

LIBRARY OF CONGRESS CATALOGING-IN-PUBLICATION DATA
Gray, Susan Heinrichs.
  Apatosaurus / by Susan H. Gray; illustrated by Robert Squier.
    p. cm.—(Introducing dinosaurs)
  Includes bibliographical references and index.
  ISBN 978-1-60253-236-6 (lib. bound: alk. paper)
  1. Apatosaurus—Juvenile literature. I. Squier, Robert, ill. II. Title. III. Series.
  QE862.S3G6922 2009
  567.913'8—dc22   2009001622

TABLE OF CONTENTS

WHAT WAS APATOSAURUS?

Apatosaurus (uh-pah-tuh-SAWR-uss) was a gigantic dinosaur. It was one of the biggest animals ever. It was as long as a basketball court. *Apatosaurus* was heavy, too. An adult weighed about as much as fifteen cars!

Apatosaurus *was very big, even for a dinosaur. Slam-dunking a basketball would have been no problem for Apatosaurus!*

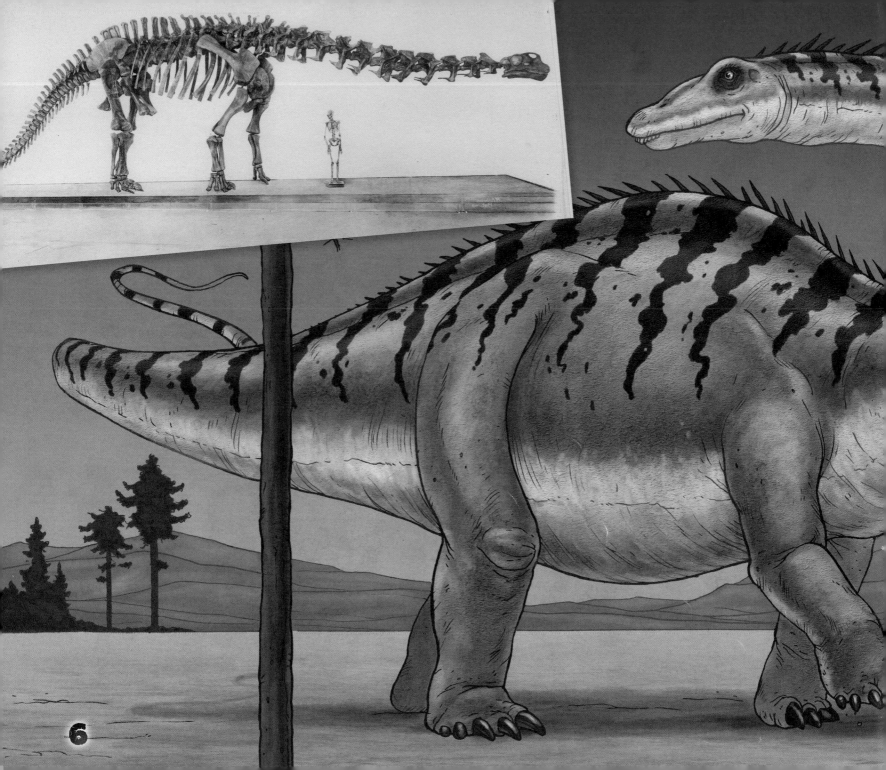

WHAT DID *APATOSAURUS* LOOK LIKE?

Apatosaurus had a long neck and a very long tail. Its legs were the size of tree trunks. It had a huge belly. *Apatosaurus* also had thick skin. This protected it from attacks by other dinosaurs.

One Apatosaurus *leg was taller than a person (top). If* Apatosaurus *lived today, it would be taller than most houses.*

The head of *Apatosaurus* was tiny for its body. Its brain was about the size of an orange. Its **nostrils** were near the top of its head. Its teeth were shaped like **blunt** pencils.

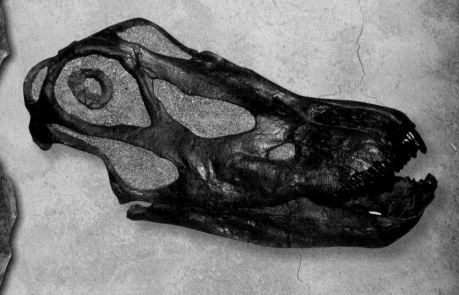

Most Apatosaurus *skulls (above) were about 2 feet (0.6 meters) long. That might seem big for a person, but it was small for Apatosaurus' huge body. Apatosaurus' teeth were useful for eating plants, but were not sharp enough for eating meat.*

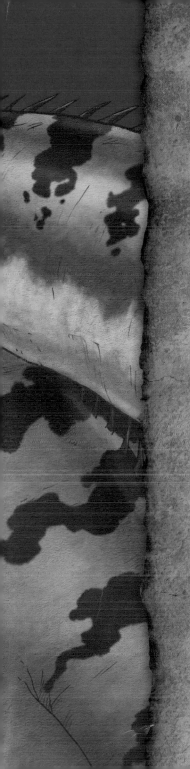

HOW DID *APATOSAURUS* GET AROUND?

Apatosaurus moved slowly. It plodded along on its big, heavy feet. It probably held its tail up off the ground.

Apatosaurus could not run quickly. That made it easy for other dinosaurs to attack it. The fierce **Allosaurus** (al-luh-SAWR-uss) sometimes went after *Apatosaurus*. But *Apatosaurus* could defend itself. It had that long tail. The tail could whip an attacker in the head. It could knock *Allosaurus* **unconscious**!

Apatosaurus *was not the best fighter. Its whiplike tail was the only way it could protect itself from attackers.*

HOW DID *APATOSAURUS* SPEND ITS TIME?

Apatosaurus spent most of its time eating. It did not hunt other dinosaurs. It ate plants instead.

Apatosaurus ate sticks and leaves. It ate pine needles and pinecones. It ate ferns and bushes.

These gingko leaves would have been a tasty meal for Apatosaurus. *It's thought that Apatosaurus* had thick lips that helped it gather leaves.

13

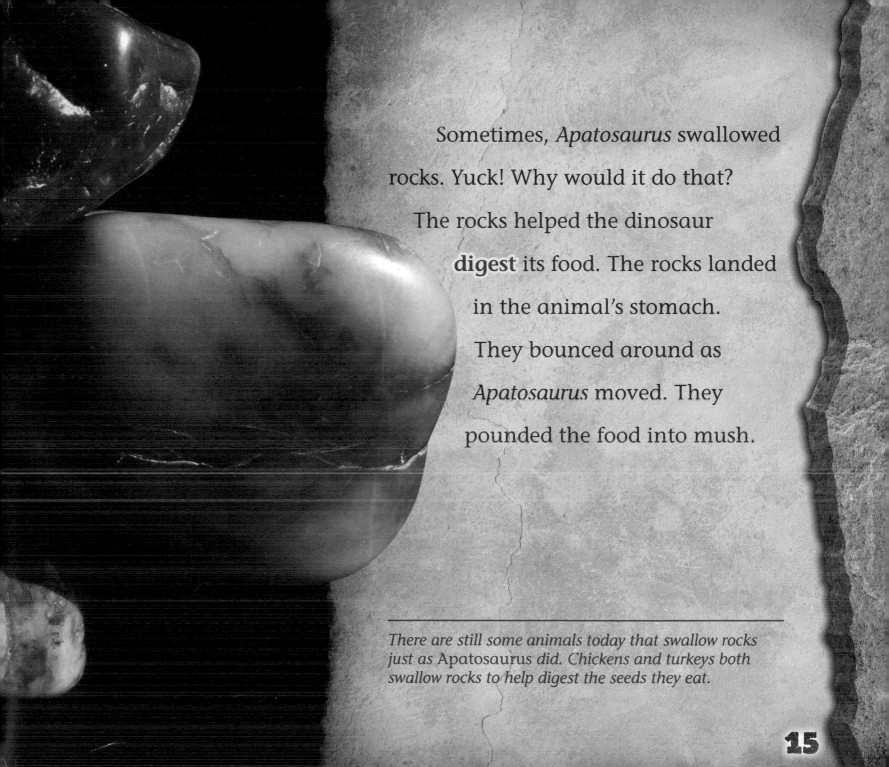

Sometimes, *Apatosaurus* swallowed rocks. Yuck! Why would it do that? The rocks helped the dinosaur **digest** its food. The rocks landed in the animal's stomach. They bounced around as *Apatosaurus* moved. They pounded the food into mush.

There are still some animals today that swallow rocks just as Apatosaurus *did. Chickens and turkeys both swallow rocks to help digest the seeds they eat.*

HOW DO WE KNOW ABOUT APATOSAURUS?

We know about *Apatosaurus* because of its **fossils**. Fossils are things that dead animals and plants have left behind. The dinosaurs died out many years ago. But some of their bones, teeth, and claws have been preserved, or saved, as fossils.

These Apatosaurus *leg bones (above) were shown at a museum in New York. These fossilized* Apatosaurus *bones (right) can be seen at the Dinosaur National Monument Quarry in Utah. The fossils found there have helped us learn much about* Apatosaurus.

Dinosaur nests and eggs were also preserved. **Scientists** find these fossils in the ground.

So far, scientists have found *Apatosaurus* bones and teeth. They have found its footprints. They have even found the rocks from its stomach!

Fossils of dinosaur nests help scientists understand how Apatosaurus babies might have been born (left). Scientists can also learn how dinosaurs lived and how fast they moved from a fossilized dinosaur footprint (above).

WHERE HAVE APATOSAURUS BONES BEEN FOUND?

Montana

Wyoming

Utah

NORTH AMERICA

Oklahoma

Colorado

EUROPE

ASIA

Atlantic Ocean

AFRICA

Pacific Ocean

SOUTH AMERICA

Indian Ocean

AUSTRALIA

Map Key

Where *Apatosaurus* bones have been found

Southern Ocean

WHO FINDS THE BONES?

Fossil hunters find dinosaur bones. Some fossil hunters are scientists. Others are people who hunt fossils for fun. They go to areas where dinosaurs once lived. They find bones in rocky places, in mountainsides, and in deserts.

When fossil hunters discover dinosaur bones, they get busy. They use picks to chip rocks away from the fossils. They use small brushes to sweep off any dirt. They take pictures of the fossils. They also write notes about where the fossils were found. They want to remember everything!

Fossil hunters use many tools to dig up fossils. It is very important to use the right tools so the fossils do not get damaged.

GLOSSARY

Allosaurus (*al-luh-SAWR-uss*) *Allosaurus* was a big, meat-eating dinosaur.

Apatosaurus (*uh-pah-tuh-SAWR-uss*) *Apatosaurus* was one of the largest dinosaurs that ever lived.

blunt (*BLUHNT*) Blunt things are those that are not sharp.

digest (*dye-JEST*) To digest food means to break it down into smaller pieces.

fossils (*FOSS-ullz*) Fossils are preserved parts of plants and animals that died long ago.

nostrils (*NOSS-trullz*) The nostrils are the openings in the nose.

scientists (*SY-un-tists*) Scientists are people who study how things work through observations and experiments.

unconscious (*un-KON-shuss*) An unconscious animal is one that has passed out and cannot think or act.

BOOKS

Birch, Robin. *Long-necked Dinosaurs*.
New York: Chelsea House Publishers, 2008.

Landau, Elaine. *Apatosaurus*.
New York: Scholastic, 2007.

Mattern, Joanne. *Apatosaurus*. Pleasantville, NY:
Weekly Reader Early Learning Library, 2007.

Matthews, Rupert. *Apatosaurus*.
Chicago: Heinemann Library, 2004.

WEB SITES

Visit our Web site for lots of links about *Apatosaurus*:
CHILDSWORLD.COM/LINKS

Note to Parents, Teachers, and Librarians: We routinely verify our Web links to make sure they are safe, active sites—so encourage your readers to check them out!

INDEX

ABOUT THE AUTHOR

Susan Gray has written more than ninety books for children. She especially likes to write about animals. Susan lives in Cabot, Arkansas, with her husband, Michael, and many pets.

ABOUT THE ILLUSTRATOR

Robert Squier has been drawing dinosaurs ever since he could hold a crayon. Today, instead of using crayons, he uses pencils, paint, and the computer. Robert lives in New Hampshire with his wife, Jessica, and a house full of dinosaur toys. *Stegosaurus* is his favorite dinosaur.